SO-AZF-837

WANTED!

FAMOUS OUTLAWS

BUTCH CASSIDY

AND THE SUNDANCE KID

NOTORIOUS OUTLAWS OF THE WEST

TIM COOKE

Gareth Stevens
PUBLISHING

Please visit our website, **www.garethstevens.com**.
For a free color catalog of all our high-quality books,
call toll-free 1-800-542-2595 or fax 1-877-542-2596.

Library of Congress Cataloging-in-Publication Data

Cooke, Tim, 1961-
Butch Cassidy and the Sundance Kid : notorious outlaws of the west / Tim Cooke.
     pages cm. — (Wanted! : Famous Outlaws)
Includes bibliographical references and index.
ISBN 978-1-4824-4255-7 (pbk.)
ISBN 978-1-4824-4256-4 (6 pack)
ISBN 978-1-4824-4257-1 (library binding)
1. Cassidy, Butch, 1866—-Juvenile literature. 2. Sundance Kid—Juvenile literature.
3. Outlaws—West (U.S.)—Biography—Juvenile literature. 4. Crime—West (U.S.)—History—Juvenile literature.
5. West (U.S.)—History—Juvenile literature. 6. West (U.S.)—Biography—Juvenile literature. I. Title.
F595.C362C66 2016
364.1552092—dc23
[B]

2015025565

Published in 2016 by
Gareth Stevens Publishing
111 East 14th Street, Suite 349
New York, NY 10003

© 2016 Brown Bear Books Ltd

For Brown Bear Books Ltd:
Editorial Director: Lindsey Lowe
Managing Editor: Tim Cooke
Children's Publisher: Anne O'Daly
Design Manager: Keith Davis
Designer: Melissa Roskell
Picture Manager: Sophie Mortimer

Picture Credits: Front Cover: Library of Congress. Alamy: Room the Agency 15; Corbis: Patrick Bennett 35, Johathan Blair
40; Daily Graphic: 6; Esmoraca & Mojinete Bolivia: 38; Getty Images: the Denver Post 39, Underwood Archives 27; Paul
Hermans: 20; Jerrye and Roy Klotz: 14; Karen Jensen: 8; Library of Congress: 4, 11, 12, 16, 19, 21, 22, 24, 25, 28, 29, 32, 36, 44;
Kim MacQuarrie: 41; Robert Hunt Library: 13, 45; Shutterstock: 34, John Pablo Bueno 37, Everett Historical 17, Mariuz S.
Jurgielewicz 18, Marzolino 5, Meunierd 23, Lincoln Rogers 31, Joseph Sohm 30 sunsinger 33, Vlad Turchenko 7; Topfoto:
10, 42; Twentieth Century Fox: 43; Barbara Whitney: 9.

Brown Bear Books has made every attempt to contact the copyright holders.
If anyone has any information please contact licensing@brownbearbooks.co.uk

Manufactured in the United States of America

CPSIA compliance information: Batch #CW16GS. For further information contact Gareth Stevens, New York, New York at 1-800-542-2595.

CONTENTS

INTRODUCTION

Butch Cassidy was a famous bank robber and train robber. He led the Wild Bunch, one of the most feared gangs of the West.

The Wild Bunch stole from banks, railroads, and mining companies. Butch said he never shot anyone. Some people admired him. They saw him as an outlaw standing up for the rights of individuals against big business.

Butch Cassidy's real name was Robert Leroy Parker. He was born in Beaver, Utah, on April 13, 1866. Utah had only been settled by white

Mormon settlers traveled west to Utah to escape hostility from people in the east. Mormon beliefs had made them unpopular.

The Mormon pioneers coming off Big Mountain into Mountain Dell. July 1847.

The Mormons built Salt Lake City in the desert of Utah. Conditions there were tough.

Americans about 20 years earlier. It was still part of the **frontier**. Life in Utah was hard. There was little law and order.

A Mormon upbringing

Most settlers in Utah territory were Mormons. They included Robert Leroy Parker's parents. Mormons belong to the Church of Jesus Christ of Latter-day Saints. The church had been founded by Joseph Smith in New York State in 1830. Its teachings included the belief that a man could have more than one wife. Such an unusual belief made Mormons unpopular with non-Mormons.

Frontier The border area between settled land and the wilderness beyond.

This cartoon from 1883 shows a Mormon defying Uncle Sam. It poked fun at the Mormons' wish to follow their own laws.

The US government tried to ban the religion, and some Mormons were attacked. Smith was murdered by a mob in 1844. Two years later, a new leader named Brigham Young led the Mormons west. They wanted to find a place where they could practice their religion free from persecution. They walked thousands of miles across the Plains and through the Rocky Mountains, until they reached the Great Salt Lake Basin in Utah, where they settled.

Robert Leroy Parker's grandfather had moved to the United States from England. He became a Mormon minister and led his family on the **migration** westward.

A hard life

Most Mormon families were farmers. The Great Salt Lake Basin was not suited to farming, however. The early pioneers had to **irrigate** the land to make it suitable for planting crops. The Mormon community grew quickly.

When the Mormons arrived on July 24, 1847, Utah was part of Mexico. The next year, it became part of the United States after the Mexican–American War (1846–48). The Mormons continued to follow their own laws, however. Robert Leroy Parker may not have taken US laws seriously. That may have influenced his later decision to become an outlaw.

Salt Lake City is still the headquarters of the Mormon faith and the state capital of Utah.

Migration The movement of a group of people from one place to another.

Irrigate To supply water to crops through artificial channels.

Utah Upbringing

Robert Leroy Parker grew up in a small cabin in a remote valley where his family had built a homestead.

The Parkers moved to this small cabin near Circleville in Utah.

Robert was the eldest of 13 brothers and sisters. He was known as Bob. He spent the early part of his life in Circleville, Utah, close to what is now Bryce Canyon National Park. He was brought up by his mother, Ann, and his father, Maxi. The family was poor and struggled to support itself.

Life of struggle

When Bob was a young boy, his father managed to buy a ranch 12 miles (19 km) from Circleville. The family lived there in a remote two-roomed cabin. Bob worked on the ranch with his father, but they struggled to make a living. During their first year on

Utah's landscape was spectacular but it was poor for farming. The Parkers struggled to make a living from it.

the farm, bad weather ruined the harvest and a cold winter killed the cattle. Things got worse after Maxi tried to claim more land. The local Mormon minister gave the land to another **homesteader**. The 13-year-old Bob and his parents had to find work off the ranch to earn money. Bob worked on other ranches across western Utah.

LIKEABLE OUTLAW

Even as a young man, Robert Parker was very popular. He was known for his sense of humor, friendly manner, and charming personality. Such qualities helped him to remain a popular figure even after he became an outlaw.

Homesteader Someone who claims public land to build a home.

Cowboy Hero

In 1879 Robert Leroy Parker met a cowboy named Mike Cassidy. Parker changed his surname to Cassidy in honor of his new hero.

Mike Cassidy was an expert cowboy. He took Robert Parker under his wing.

Bob Parker first met Mike Cassidy when they both worked on the same ranch. Cassidy taught the young Bob how to ride a horse, how to shoot a gun, and how to rope, **brand**, and **rustle** cattle. By the time he was 16, Bob was said to be the best shot in Circleville. He was also skilled at taming wild horses so they could be ridden.

A thief

Cassidy was also a horse rustler. He took Bob Parker on his raids. At night, the pair stole horses from ranches near the Utah state border. They took the horses over the border. At the time, law enforcement was organized by each state. Lawmen from Utah could not chase them into another state. Cassidy and Parker could sell the horses in another state without fear of being caught.

Bob started calling himself "Cassidy." He changed his first name to George, and later to Butch. There are two stories about how he got the name "Butch." One story says it was because he once worked as a butcher. In the other story, Mike Cassidy had a rifle. He called it "the Butcher" because of its fierce **recoil**. One day, Bob fired the rifle and was knocked back into a pond. Mike Cassidy gave him the name "Butch" in memory of the occasion!

Cassidy's first crime was taking a pair of jeans from a store. He is said to have left a note promising to pay for the jeans.

Brand An identification mark burned onto an animal.

Rustle To round up and steal horses or cattle.

Recoil The snap back of a gun when it is fired.

Focus: Cowboy Life

Butch Cassidy's life as a cowboy was not very promising. Cowboy life was hard and poorly paid.

Cowboys gather on a ranch for an outdoor meal during the spring cattle roundup.

Cowboys moved around to find work. Their job depended on the season. During the winter, they worked on ranches, making sure the cattle did not wander too far. In spring, they rounded up the cattle and rescued cows that had become lost or trapped in bogs. During the summer months, they drove the cattle on long trails to the railroads and to market.

On the trail

On the cattle trails, cowboys rode all day, slept outside at night, and lived on beef, biscuits, beans, and black coffee. The work was hard. There could be up to 15,000 cattle in a herd, and the herd had to cover an average of 15 miles (24 km) each day. As many as 12 cowboys controlled each herd. They all had to be highly skilled horse riders.

Because their life was so hard, cowboys were usually young. The average age was 24. Like the Native Americans, cowboys were **nomads** who traveled light. They relied entirely on the cattle for their livelihood and food, much as the Native Americans relied on the buffalo.

DIFFERENT ROLES

Cowboys had different jobs on the trail. The "wrangler" looked after the horses. The "point" rode at the front of the cattle herd. He kept lookout and turned the herd in the right direction. The "drag" chased up any cattle that fell behind.

A cowboy holds his lasso ready to rope any cattle escaping from the herd during a drive in 1902.

Nomads People who move around and have no permanent home.

A Life of Crime

Around the age of 18, Butch moved to Colorado and Wyoming. He also moved on from rustling to robbery.

The San Miguel Valley Bank building still stands in Telluride. It was robbed by the McCarty gang in 1889.

On June 14, 1889, four men robbed the San Miguel Valley Bank in the town of Telluride, Colorado. They got away with $20,750 (about $550,000 in today's money). The local newspapers identified two of the robbers as the McCarty brothers, Tom and Bill. Experts now also think this was Butch Cassidy's first bank robbery.

Outlaw hideouts

The gang had left fresh horses along their getaway route, so they could change horses as they went. This helped them outrun the tired horses of the **posse** that chased them. The robbers fled to an isolated **hideout** in southeastern Utah named

Robber's Roost. The hideout was very remote. Law enforcement officials did not even know it existed until after Cassidy's death. Cassidy and his gang used Robber's Roost to hide after most of their robberies.

In 1890, Cassidy bought a ranch in Dubois, Wyoming. He may have paid for it with money he had stolen. The ranch was near another isolated hideaway, the Hole-in-the-Wall. Outlaws could hide in the remote canyon for months at a time.

Robber's Roost was a canyon with caves and lookout points. Very few outsiders went there, making it a good place for outlaws to hide.

THE HOLE-IN-THE-WALL

Different gangs used the Hole-in-the-Wall for around 50 years, from the 1860s to 1910. Robbers headed to the remote Wyoming canyon after a robbery to hide from the forces of the law. The outlaws who used it included Butch Cassidy and other members of his gang, the Wild Bunch.

Posse A group of citizens helping a sheriff.

Hideout A place used to hide from other people.

A Spell in Prison

In 1892, the law caught up with Butch Cassidy. He was finally found guilty of stealing a horse and put in jail.

The state prison in Laramie was intended to hold Wyoming's most serious criminals.

Butch Cassidy was arrested and charged with stealing a horse. His defense was that he had bought the horse from a rustler without knowing it was stolen. Cassidy was tried at Lander, Wyoming, and was found guilty. Long legal delays meant he was not sentenced until 1894. He was given two years in Wyoming's State **Penitentiary** in Laramie. According to one story, Cassidy asked the local sheriff if he could go home for the night if he

This photo of Cassidy was taken in jail. He was prisoner number 187.

promised to return the next day. The sheriff was said to have agreed, and also to have lent Cassidy a horse. Cassidy did return the following day, as promised, and began his sentence.

A model prisoner

After serving 18 months of his two-year sentence, Cassidy wrote to Wyoming's Governor William P. Richards. He asked to be released early. Cassidy had been well behaved, so the governor agreed as long as Cassidy promised to stay out of trouble. However, after his release on January 19, 1896, Cassidy returned to the Hole-in-the-Wall. He was ready to put together his own gang and commit more robberies.

GETTING AWAY WITH IT

The 18 months Butch Cassidy spent in the penitentiary was the only time the outlaw ever spent in jail. Cassidy was widely suspected of being involved in robbing banks and trains. However, there was never any evidence to allow the law to prosecute him.

Penitentiary A prison for people found guilty of serious crimes.

The Wild Bunch

Back at the Hole-in-the-Wall, Cassidy got together some of his closest friends to form a gang.

Winnemucca in Nevada was the scene of one of the Wild Bunch's many robberies of September 1900.

Butch Cassidy's gang included his closest friend, Elzy Lay. They had met when they were both working as ranch hands. The gang also included Harry Longabaugh, who later traveled with Cassidy to South America. Longabaugh's nickname was the Sundance Kid. Some of the other outlaws also had nicknames. Harvey Logan's was Kid Curry.

The number of gang members went up and down. There were around 30 members in all, but most of them were only in the gang for one or two robberies. At least two women also took part in the gang's raids: Laura Bullion and Camilla Hanks.

Bad reputation

The gang started out mainly robbing banks. Although it was later named the Wild Bunch, the outlaws tried to avoid shooting people. Cassidy claimed that he had never killed anyone.

Jesse Linsley was one of many gang members who took part in Wild Bunch robberies.

The gang was at its most active between 1896 and 1901. No one knows how many crimes it carried out, nor how many Butch Cassidy was actually involved in. But the **reputation** of the Wild Bunch was firmly established. Cassidy and the gang were wanted outlaws with prices on their heads.

Reputation How someone or something is judged by the general public.

Train Robbers

The Wild Bunch started off robbing banks in 1896. They soon turned their attention to the mines and railroads of the West.

When the Wild Bunch robbed this bank in Montpelier, a deputy chased them by bicycle.

On August 13, 1896, the Wild Bunch robbed a bank in Montpelier, Idaho. They got away with $7,000 (about $200,000 in today's money). But Cassidy wanted to make more money. He decided to target the mining companies and railroads. They were better guarded than banks, so robbing them was more risky. Cassidy thought the higher profits made it worth taking the risk.

Castle Gate

Butch Cassidy usually avoided crimes in Utah in case someone recognized him. However, he made an exception when he targeted the Pleasant Valley Coal Company in Castle Gate, Utah. Money to pay the miners came by train. The company was worried that the train might be robbed. It altered the time the train arrived each day so robbers wouldn't know the timetable. Cassidy watched the train arrive every day for a week. Finally, on April 21, 1897, Cassidy and a **sidekick**—probably Elzy Lay—watched the money being carried off the train in heavy bags. They held up the company paymaster, E. L. Carpenter. Carpenter handed over the money, but in the confusion Cassidy's horse was **spooked**. It ran off, so Cassidy had to flee on foot. Nevertheless, he got away with $8,800 ($260,000 in today's money).

MINING IN THE WEST

Utah and other states in the West had rich supplies of coal and other minerals. Many companies opened mines to dig minerals out of the ground. The mines were very remote. They relied on railroads to transport the minerals. Railroads also brought money and supplies for the miners.

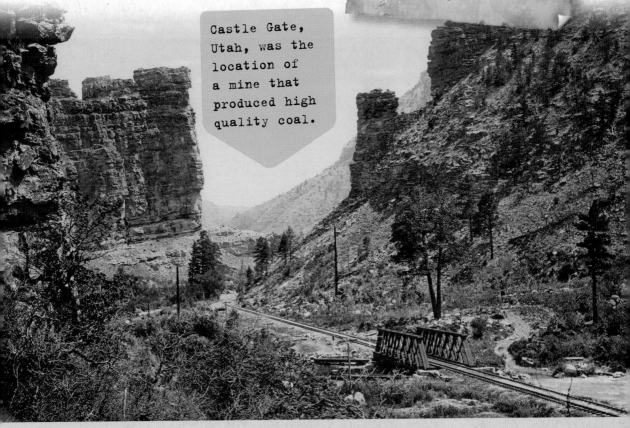

Castle Gate, Utah, was the location of a mine that produced high quality coal.

Sidekick An assistant who helps a person in charge.

Spooked Scared.

THE GREAT TRAIN ROBBERY

SENSATIONAL AND STARTLING "HOLD UP" OF THE "GOLD EXPRESS," BY FAMOUS WESTERN OUTLAWS.

People were fascinated by train robberies. This poster advertised a theatrical performance of a robbery.

Cassidy had planned the Castle Gate **payroll** robbery carefully. He had cut the telegraph wires so Carpenter could not raise the alarm. Cassidy and Lay got away, despite being chased by a posse. They had left fresh horses along their route and knew the land well. That helped them reach Robber's Roost, where they spent the next three months in the hideout.

A switch to trains

Between 1899 and 1901, Cassidy and the Wild Bunch carried out at least five train robberies in Wyoming, Oregon, New Mexico, and Montana. They flagged down a train, then held it up at gunpoint. They always robbed the safe in the mail car, never the passengers. In one train robbery on June 2, 1899, the gang got away with as much as $60,000 (almost $1.8 million in today's money).

MAJOR WILD BUNCH ROBBERIES

PLACE	DATE	AMOUNT
Montpelier, Idaho	August 13, 1896	$7,165
Castle Gate, Utah	April 21, 1897	$8,800
Wilcox, Wyoming	June 2, 1899	$60,000
Folsom, New Mexico	July 11, 1899	$70,000
Tipton, Wyoming	August 29, 1900	$55,000
Winnemucca, New Mexico	September 19, 1900	$32,000
Exter, Montana	July 3, 1901	$65,000

As the Wild Bunch committed more crimes, bigger rewards were offered for their capture.

Democratic outlaws

The **booty** from a robbery was always divided fairly. Half went to pay anyone who had helped the gang, such as railroad employees, bank cashiers, or telegraph operators. The other half was divided equally between all members of the Wild Bunch, whatever the size of their role in the robbery.

$4,000 Reward

WILL BE PAID FOR THE CAPTURE OF ROBERT LEROY PARKER

DEAD OR ALIVE

Age, 36 years (1901)
Weight, 165 lbs.
Complexion, Light.
Eyes, Blue.
Nationality, American.
Marks, two cut scars back of head, small scar under left eye, small brown mole calf of leg.

Height, 5 ft. 9 in.
Build, Medium.
Color of hair, Flaxen.
Mustache, sandy if any.
Occupation, Cowboy, Rustler.
Criminal occupation, bank robber & Highwayman, cattle and horse thief.

ROBERT LEROY PARKER
ALIAS
"BUTCH" CASSIDY

Is known as a criminal principally in Wyoming, Utah, Idaho, Colorado & Nevada and has served time in Wyoming State Penitentiary at Laramie for grand larceny, but was pardoned January 19, 1896. Wanted for robbery First National Bank, WINNEMUCCA, NEVADA, September 19, 1900.

Payroll Money used by a company to pay the wages of its workers.

Booty Valuable stolen goods.

The Pinkertons

In desperation, railroad bosses hired the Pinkerton National Detective Agency to catch the outlaws.

Pinkerton's agents like these traveled on trains in the West to protect them from robbery.

On June 2, 1899, the Wild Bunch robbed a train near Wilcox, Wyoming. As the gang made its getaway, Sheriff Joe Hazen was shot dead. A group of bankers, businessmen, and railroad owners decided to take action. They hired the Pinkerton National Detective Agency. The agency had first made its name when it had foiled a plot to kill **president-elect** Abraham Lincoln in 1860.

The Pinkerton agency sent Charlie Siringo to hunt down Butch Cassidy and his gang. Siringo was one of their best agents. He worked with another Pinkerton employee named Tom Horn.

Horn was known to be a killer for hire. Siringo and Horn used different methods to try to locate the Wild Bunch. Horn used threats and violence. Siringo was more crafty. He became friendly with a woman who knew the brother of Kid Curry. Curry was a member of the Wild Bunch.

A long pursuit

Pinkerton agents pursued Butch Cassidy and his gang for the next 10 years. They collected information about Cassidy, the Sundance Kid, and Sundance's girlfriend, Etta Place. Their information led to the arrest of a number of members of the Wild Bunch. In the end, the agency's determination to catch the outlaws persuaded Cassidy and the Sundance Kid to try to give up their life of crime.

Charlie Siringo posed as an outlaw to get himself close to the Wild Bunch.

A WORLD FIRST

The Pinkerton detective agency was the first detective agency in the world. It was founded by Scotsman Allan Pinkerton in Chicago in 1850. Its badge was an open eye with the motto "We Never Sleep." By 1869, the Pinkerton agency employed about 10,000 people.

President-elect Someone who has won a presidential election but not yet taken office as president.

25

Under Pursuit

Butch Cassidy began to realize that the days of the Wild Bunch were numbered. Increasingly, gang members were being injured or arrested and jailed.

Five leading members of the Wild Bunch (from left to right): Harry Longabaugh, William Carver, Ben Kilpatrick, Harvey Logan, and Butch Cassidy.

Cassidy always claimed that he had never killed a man during a raid. That was not true of other members of the Wild Bunch. The gang robbed a train near Folsom, New Mexico, in July 1899. A posse cornered Elzy Lay, Will Carver, Kid Curry, and Sam Ketchum. In the gunfight that followed, the outlaws killed the sheriff and his deputy. Elzy Lay was wounded but escaped. Ketchum was captured. He died of his wounds in jail.

On the run

Elzy Lay was soon captured. He was found guilty of the killings and sent to jail in New Mexico for life. Lay's capture made Cassidy start to think about whether he should continue his life of crime.

Many different groups were closing in on the Wild Bunch. Their usual hideouts were no longer safe. The gang had to keep moving. They required all their **survival skills** to stay alive. They could not light a fire for fear of being spotted; they could not risk staying too long in one place. The outlaws carried the money from their robberies—but they had nowhere to spend it.

KID CURRY

After the Folsom robbery, Pinkerton agents chased Kid Curry all the way to Arkansas. Curry was wanted for 15 murders, but he may have killed twice that many men. According to some stories, his luck finally ran out in 1904 after he robbed a train in Colorado. Wounded during a gunfight, he took his own life rather than go back to jail.

A posse loads horses onto a railcar as they set out in pursuit of the Wild Bunch.

Survival skills Skills that enable people to find food and shelter in wilderness areas.

Plea for Amnesty

After Elzy Lay was arrested in 1899, Butch Cassidy decided to try to get out of his life of crime. He came up with a surprising solution.

Utah governor Heber Wells (far right) meets President Theodore Roosevelt (center) in 1903.

In 1900, Cassidy went to see Judge Orlando W. Powers in Utah. He asked the judge to ask Utah's governor, Heber Wells, to grant him an **amnesty**. In exchange Cassidy would give up crime. When the judge could not help, Cassidy went directly to Heber Wells. He agreed to give Cassidy an amnesty as long as he had never been accused of murder. When he discovered that Cassidy was wanted for murder he withdrew his offer of amnesty.

Close to a deal

Cassidy was not put off. He went back to Judge Powers, who this time decided to help. Powers arranged for Cassidy to meet officials from the

Union Pacific Railroad. In exchange for no longer robbing their trains, the railroad company planned to offer Cassidy a job as a train guard. The plan fell through when the railroad officials were delayed by bad weather and were late for the meeting.

Cassidy thought he had been deliberately ignored. After a day of waiting, he left the meeting place. His attempt to give up his life of crime had failed. He decided to keep on robbing trains.

WEARY OF CRIME

Cassidy told Judge Powers he was tired of always hiding from the law. He said, "You'll never know what it means to be forever on the dodge."

Edward Harriman (right) ran the Union Pacific Railroad. He was ready to make a deal with Cassidy.

Amnesty An official pardon for a crime.

Focus: End of the Wild West

By the late 19th century, the West was changing. Railroads and mining had opened up the frontier.

State capitols, like that of Nevada in Carson City, were symbols of the coming of law and order to the West.

In the old Wild West, people used guns to settle disputes. Now law and order were taking over. Sheriffs enforced laws, but it was difficult for them to protect populations spread over vast areas. People often took the law into their own hands. They formed **vigilante** groups to fight crime. Associations were formed to solve issues of land ownership. As the railroads spread farther west, they hired their own guards to protect their trains.

Nowhere to run

For outlaws like the Wild Bunch, the Wild West was disappearing as the 19th century came to a close. Agencies, such as the Pinkerton National Detective Agency, employed dedicated agents. The agents were prepared to go to any lengths to catch outlaws.

The legal system in the West was improving. Police forces worked in larger towns. They enforced laws against carrying concealed weapons, being drunk in public, or gambling. Frontier marshals enforced laws in small communities. With more judges to try cases, and better jails to hold criminals, it was clear that crime was no longer an easy way to make money in the West.

Despite the end of the Wild West, Wild West shows remain popular today.

LAW AND ORDER

Pinkerton's detective agency was not the only group bringing law and order to the West. Banks and railroads began to use other private detectives. Bounty hunters caught outlaws for bounty, or reward money. Volunteers from the US Cavalry also chased outlaws.

Vigilante Someone who takes responsibility for enforcing the law, even though they have no authority.

Looking for a New Life

With Pinkerton's detectives hot on his trail, Butch Cassidy fled to New York City and then to South America.

The Sundance Kid, photographed with Etta Place before moving to Argentina.

Butch Cassidy had enough money to plan a fresh start away from the West. In New York, he met up with the Sundance Kid. The Kid had brought his girlfriend, Etta Place, along. Cassidy used the **alias** Jim Ryan, while Sundance and Etta called themselves Mr. and Mrs. Harry Place.

Going south

On February 20, 1901, the former outlaws boarded a British steamer. They sailed to Buenos Aires in Argentina. The three then traveled farther south. In 1902, Cassidy, Sundance, and Etta settled on a large piece of land in a remote part of Patagonia, in the far south of Argentina.

Patagonia is one of the most remote regions in the Americas.

For three years, the outlaws lived as ranchers, raising sheep, cattle, and horses. Their Argentine neighbors believed that Cassidy and the Kid were brothers. But the Pinkerton agency had not given up. Agent Frank P. Dimaio traced Cassidy to Argentina. Again, the former outlaws were living on borrowed time.

SETTLING DOWN

In March 1902, Sundance walked into a bank in Buenos Aires in Argentina. He deposited over $12,000 in cash. On April 2, Cassidy and Sundance applied to settle in Cholila, Argentina. Cassidy had fled about 6,000 miles (9,655 km) from the scenes of his crimes in the American West.

Alias A false identity or name.

Butch and Sundance

After three years living quietly on their ranch, Butch and Sundance returned to their old life of crime.

No one knows why the outlaws gave up ranching in Patagonia for a new life in crime.

Why Butch and Sundance gave up their peaceful lives is a mystery. One **theory** is that an American named A. P. Field arrived in Cholila to buy cattle. He had been a sheriff in Wyoming and recognized Cassidy. Another story is that they knew Pinkerton's agents were closing in on them.

Bank raids

On February 14, 1905, robbers held up a bank in Rio Gallegos at the very southern tip of Argentina. The criminals were probably Cassidy and Sundance, even though the town was 700 miles (1,126 km)

The three outlaws left their isolated ranch house in Cholila around summer 1906.

south of Cholila. The two men may have been helped by Kid Curry. Curry had escaped from jail in 1902. He may have traveled south, although some reports say he had killed himself after a robbery in Colorado in 1904.

In March 1906, Cassidy and Sundance stole $20,000 from a bank in Mercedes in Uruguay. Etta stayed in the street to mind the horses. A third robber might have been Kid Curry. There were other bank raids in Argentina, but the identity of the raiders was never confirmed. In any case, Butch and Sundance sold their ranch and left Cholila for good.

A CRIME TOO FAR?

Among other crimes, Butch Cassidy and the Sundance Kid were accused of killing a man in Arroyo Pescado, Argentina, in 1910. There were two problems with the accusation. First, killing was not their style. Second, they are thought to have been dead by then.

Theory A suggested explanation for something.

Lying Low

Sometime in 1906, Cassidy and Sundance decided to go their separate ways. But they would soon meet up again.

The Sundance Kid returned to the United States with Etta Place. The two traveled to San Francisco. Etta had grown tired of their life in South America, but no one really knows why.

Sundance and Etta Place moved to San Francisco at the time when the city was being rebuilt following an earthquake in April 1906.

A new identity

Meanwhile, Butch Cassidy moved across the border from Argentina to Bolivia and renamed himself James "Santiago" Maxwell. He got a job at the Concordia tin mine near the village of Tres

Cruces, 90 miles (145 km) southeast of the Bolivian capital, La Paz. Cassidy quickly became known as an excellent worker. He was put in charge of the mine's payroll.

The Sundance Kid did not stay in the United States for long. The Pinkerton detectives many have been on his trail. He made his way to the tin mine in Concordia. Cassidy got him a job. At the mine, the outlaws became friends with an engineer named Percy Seibert. He would play a crucial role in the final chapter of Butch and Sundance's lives.

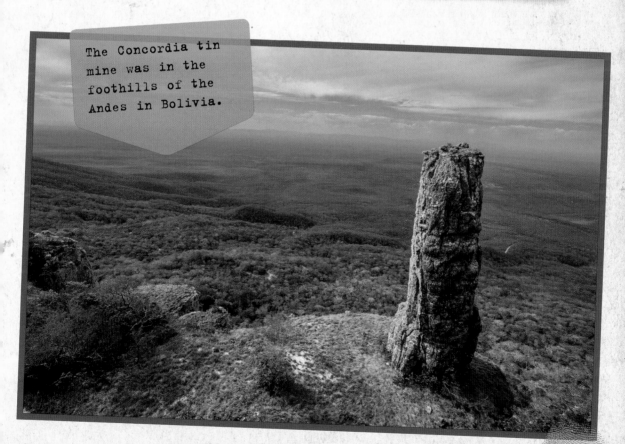

The Concordia tin mine was in the foothills of the Andes in Bolivia.

The Final Shootout

Mystery surrounds what became of Butch Cassidy. According to his friend Percy Seibert, he carried out one last robbery before reaching a violent end.

San Vicente today is still a mining settlement high in the Bolivian Andes.

On November 3, 1909, robbers stole the payroll of the Aramayo mine in southern Bolivia. Three days later, two American men arrived in the mining village of San Vicente. They took lodgings in a boarding house. A witness saw that their mule was marked with the brand of the Aramayo mine. He told a Bolivian military patrol about the mule.

What happened next?

There are different accounts about what happened next. One account is that a soldier entered the house where Cassidy and Sundance were staying and was shot dead by Cassidy. Two other soldiers opened fire on the house. Meanwhile, the military captain ordered the villagers to surround the building so the **fugitives** could not escape during the night. In one story, Sundance rushed outside to grab a rifle but was shot. Cassidy was said to have rescued him, but was also shot. They went back inside. There were screams from the house and then silence.

A grim discovery

When the soldiers entered the house the next morning, they found both men dead. From the look of their wounds, they thought Cassidy must have killed Sundance before turning his gun on himself.

The outlaws died in the small boarding house where they were staying.

Fugitives People who are in hiding or who have escaped from the law.

Did the Outlaws Survive?

The dead men were buried in the local cemetery. There are still different arguments about their identity.

P.N.D.a. - 1597.

No
Name Geo Cassidy alias Butch Cassidy alias
Alias Ingerfield right name Robt. Parker
Age 32 Height 5.9" Weight 165
Complexion Light Hair Flaxen
Eyes Blue Beard ___ Teeth ___
Nationality American
Marks and Scars 2 cut scars back head
Small red scar under left eye.
eyes deep set. Small brown
mole calf of leg.
Arrested for Grd. Lar. Fremont Co. Wyo.
Remarks July-15-94. Pardoned Jan 19-96
by Gov. Richards
Home is in Circle Valley. Utah
Sandy beard + Mustache if any.
8166
- 44

There are few photographs of Butch Cassidy, so identifying the outlaw relied on notes like these.

Newspaper reports about the shootout in Bolivia did not refer to the bandits by name. The dead men were simply listed as "unknown." But at about the same time as the two men were shot in San Vicente, Cassidy and Sundance disappeared. Mail sent to Sundance in 1909 went unanswered.

Years later journalists began to link Butch Cassidy and the Sundance Kid to the shootout in San Vicente. In 1930 Percy Seibert, their friend from the Bolivian tin mine, claimed that he had identified the dead men as Butch and Sundance.

Other theories

However, since 1908 the identity of the dead robbers has been fiercely debated. Some people claim that Seibert falsely identified the dead men to give his friends a chance to escape and start a new

Author William T. Phillips wrote *The Bandit Invincible*, a life story of Butch Cassidy. Some people claim that he actually was the outlaw.

UNCERTAIN IDENTITY

No one has photographed the two bodies buried in San Vicente's cemetery. In 1991 the tomb was opened and **DNA** samples were taken from the remains. The samples only added to the confusion and mystery. They showed that one set of remains belonged to a German miner.

life. Law officials would stop looking for them if they thought they were dead.

Cassidy's sister, Lula, later claimed that he visited her in 1925. There were other reports of sightings of Cassidy and Sundance across the West long after they were said to be dead. A man named William T. Phillips wrote a book about Cassidy that seemed so accurate some people believed Phillips was really Cassidy.

DNA A chemical that holds genetic information.

Focus: The Outlaws' Legacy

The question of how Butch and Sundance died has added to the mystery that surrounds them.

Butch Cassidy's sister, Lula, meets actors Paul Newman (left) and Robert Redford during the filming of the 1969 movie about Butch and Sundance.

In the eyes of the law, Cassidy and Sundance were nothing but robbers. However, in the eyes of many people they were **romantic** outlaws. They only stole from institutions such as banks, railroads, and mining companies who could afford it.

A popular hero

The story that Cassidy and Sundance had died in Bolivia in 1908 began with an interview given by their friend, Percy Seibert, in 1930. In 1975, Cassidy's sister, Lula, claimed that Cassidy had survived and had visited her. With no proof either way, people have made up their own minds about how Cassidy and Sundance died—or how they survived.

Books and movies added to the mystery. The most famous movie was the 1969 *Butch Cassidy and the Sundance Kid*. It starred Paul Newman (as Cassidy) and Robert Redford (as Sundance). The movie reinforced the idea that the two men were heroes fighting against the cold, unfeeling banks and railroads.

AN ODD COUPLE

Today people often think of Butch and Sundance together. That is mainly due to the movie *Butch Cassidy and the Sundance Kid*. In reality, Sundance was just another member of the Wild Bunch. Butch was more important. He was the gang's leader.

You never met a pair like Butch and The Kid

They're Taking Trains...
They're Taking Banks
And They're Taking
One Piece Of Baggage!

20th Century-Fox presents

PAUL NEWMAN
ROBERT REDFORD
KATHARINE ROSS

BUTCH CASSIDY AND THE SUNDANCE KID. A

A George Roy Hill–Paul Monash Production Co-Starring STROTHER MARTIN, JEFF COREY, HENRY JONES.
Executive Producer PAUL MONASH Produced by JOHN FOREMAN Directed by GEORGE ROY HILL Written by WILLIAM GOLDMAN
Music Composed and Conducted by BURT BACHARACH A NEWMAN-FOREMAN Presentation PANAVISION® COLOUR BY DE LUXE

The movie was one of the biggest international box-office hits of 1969.

Romantic Associated with an idealized and perfect view of reality.

ROGUES' GALLERY

Butch Cassidy had many friends and associates. Many of them belonged, at one time or another, to his notorious gang, the Wild Bunch.

Laura Bullion
1876–1961

One of a small number of women in the Wild Bunch, Laura was nicknamed "Della Rose" by the gang. In 1901, she was convicted of taking part in a train robbery with the Wild Bunch and served three and a half years in jail. After jail, she gave up crime and worked as a seamstress.

Elzy Lay
(1868–1934)

Elzy (born William Ellsworth Lay) was Cassidy's closest friend in the Wild Bunch. He was captured after the Folsom train robbery and sentenced to life imprisonment in New Mexico. After Lay helped put down a prison riot, he was pardoned in 1906. From 1916, he worked as a miner in Wyoming.

Kid Curry
(1867–1904?)

Born Harvey Logan, Curry had the reputation of being the "wildest of the Wild Bunch." He had a violent temper, which was made worse when he drank. According to legend, Kid Curry killed at least nine law enforcement officers but he was never charged with murder. He probably took his own life after a holdup in Colorado in 1904.

The Sundance Kid
(1867–1908?)

Born Harry Alonzo Longabaugh in Pennsylvania, he met Cassidy after Cassidy's release from jail in 1896. A member of the Wild Bunch, Longabaugh accompanied Cassidy to South America. The two men lived together with Longabaugh's girlfriend, Etta Place. Some people think he did not die in Bolivia but lived to an old age in Utah.

Etta Place
(c.1878–?)

Sundance's partner, Etta Place is the one of Butch Cassidy's associates about which the least is known. After she moved to San Francisco in 1906, she disappeared from the records. The one photograph of her shows a modest-looking woman. Some people claim she was once a schoolteacher.

GLOSSARY

Alias A false identity or name.

Amnesty An official pardon for a crime.

Booty Valuable stolen goods.

Brand An identification mark burned onto an animal.

DNA A chemical that holds unique genetic information about a person.

Frontier The border area between settled land and the wilderness beyond.

Fugitives People who are in hiding or who have escaped from the law.

Hideout A place used to hide from other people.

Homesteader Someone who claims public land to build a home.

Irrigate To supply water to crops through artificial channels.

Migration The movement of a group of people from one place to another.

Nomads People who move around and have no permanent home.

Payroll Money used by a company to pay its workers.

Penitentiary A prison for people found guilty of serious crimes.

Posse A group of citizens helping a sheriff.

President-elect Someone who has won a presidential election but not yet taken office as president.

Recoil The snap back of a gun when it is fired.

Reputation How someone or something is judged by the general public.

Romantic Associated with an idealized and perfect view of reality.

Rustle To round up and steal horses or cattle.

Sidekick An assistant who helps a person in charge.

Spooked Scared.

Survival skills Skills that enable people to find food and shelter in wilderness areas.

Theory A suggested explanation for something.

Vigilante Someone who takes responsibility for enforcing the law, even though they have no authority.

FURTHER RESOURCES

Books

Green, Carl R., and William Sanford. *Butch Cassidy*. Outlaws and Lawmen of the Wild West. Berkeley Hights, NJ: Enslow Publishers, Inc., 2008.

Hamilton, John. *Butch Cassidy*. Heroes & Villains of the Wild West. Minneapolis, MN: ABDO & Daughters, 1996.

Murray, Stuart. *Eyewitness Wild West*. New York: DK Children, 2005.

Price, Sean. *Crooks. Cowboys, and Characters: The Wild West*. American History Through Primary Sources. Chicago, IL: Raintree Fusion, 2007.

Sonneborn, Liz. *The Mormon Trail*. American West. New York: Franklin Watts, 2005.

Staton, Hilarie N. *Cowboys and the Wild West*. All About America. New York: Kingfisher, 2011.

Websites

http://www.eyewitnesstohistory.com/cassidy.htm
An eyewitness account of an 1899 train robbery by the Wild Bunch in Wyoming, written by a mail clerk traveling on the train.

http://www.historynet.com/butch-cassidy
A biography of Butch Cassidy, with a detailed account of his final years in South America.

http://www.utah.com/oldwest/butch_cassidy.htm
Page from Utah.com about the state's most infamous former outlaw.

http://www.history.com/news/history-lists/6-things-you-might-not-know-about-butch-cassidy
A History.com page with six surprising facts about Butch Cassidy, including the possible origins of his name.

INDEX